08/08
17.95

mitch murray's
one-liners
for
wedding
speeches

and how
to get
laughs

Britain's Top Speech Writer

mitch murray's
one-liners
for
wedding
speeches

and how to get laughs

foulsham
LONDON • NEW YORK • TORONTO • SYDNEY

foulsham

The Publishing House, Bennetts Close, Cippenham,
Slough, Berkshire, SL1 5AP, England

Foulsham books can be found in all good bookshops and direct from
www.foulsham.com

ISBN: 978-0-572-03426-9

Copyright © 2008 Mitch Murray

A CIP record for this book is available from the British Library

The moral right of the author has been asserted

Printed in Great Britain by Mackays of Chatham plc, Chatham, Kent

# Contents

Dedication

For many years, I was fortunate enough to have Bob Monkhouse as my special mentor. Bob was the most generous and supportive friend a man could have, and I was proud and delighted to dedicate the original edition of this book to him as a small gesture of appreciation for all his help and encouragement.

His enormous contribution to the world of humour has enriched us all, and I now re-dedicate this work to the loving memory of that extraordinary gentleman, the late Bob Monkhouse OBE.

# Introduction

You can't fool me! I know exactly why you've bought this book; you have a speech to make and you mustn't let them down.

You've seen others try:

- an embarrassingly drunk best man trying to tell risqué stories that nobody wants to hear …
- the groom who doesn't want to spoil his macho image by speaking affectionately about his bride …
- the father of the bride, desperately trying to hide the fact that he can't stand that swine of a new son-in-law!

You've seen their speeches fail, you've seen the guests squirm and now it's *your* turn.

You've been lumbered, haven't you? That's why you've bought this book. Admit it.

We authors are very clever. We *know* these things.

For instance, I happen to know you only have three requirements for this speech:

1 You want it to be witty.
2 You want it to be effective.
3 You want it to be *over*!

The good news is, that's exactly what your audience will want as well. I'm here to help.

Of course, as this may well be the only speech you're likely to be asked to make for several years, you won't want to start wading through a text book packed with intricate training techniques in the art of presentation and creativity; who's got time to read all that crap? I haven't even got time to *write* it.

So instead, how about this?

I'll show you how to prepare your own speech and I'll supply you with a rich selection of ideas, one-liners and quotations you may wish to include.

I'll let you in on some of my sneakier tricks of the trade: techniques designed to overcome the pitfalls of standing up and speaking in public.

I'll offer you advice on style and delivery and we'll look at the options of whether you should learn your speech or read it.

Taken together, these ideas will go a long way towards tackling the paradox that faces most public speakers at one time or another and that, suddenly, is now facing you: namely, how can you hope to instil confidence in your audience when you yourself are in imminent danger of a serious laundry problem?

At this point, you're probably tempted to skip a few pages and go straight into the section appropriate to the particular speech you have to make. I know you're anxious, but there are some important notes for you to read about first, so please stay with it for now. (Of course, if you went forward earlier and found yourself redirected to this page ... Hi there. Welcome back!)

The programme

At most weddings, the conventional programme begins with the *bride's father*, who proposes a toast to the bride and groom.

The *groom* replies and, in turn, proposes a toast to the bridesmaids.

At this point, tradition seems to reflect sexist and ageist values by assuming that the bridesmaids are either helplessly giggly and incompetent, or too young to stand up and speak without dribbling. To the rescue comes the *best man* who replies on their behalf and often proves to be … yes … giggly, incompetent *and* a dribbler!

Each one of these three speeches has its own individual character.

Our opener:

The father of the bride

The father of the bride is usually the straight man of the wedding speech set. Guests at the wedding party can be counted upon to treat his contribution with genial respect; after all, let's be fair, this sucker's picking up the tab.

Daddy is expected to say a few reasonably sober, sensitive yet witty words. He also has to include some love and affection. Now that takes *sincerity*, and if you can fake sincerity, you've got it made!

(Don't worry; I have a 'Sincerity Section' later in the book.)

Second on the bill:

The bridegroom

As if he didn't have enough to worry about on his wedding day, the bridegroom's speech is expected to be middle-of-the-road: not too schmaltzy but not too biting. He needs to be amusing, but he'd better be careful; should he upset his lovely new bride on her big day, he'll soon learn that beauty and the beast are the same person!

Finally, the star of the show ...

The best man

This guy thinks he's a wit ... and he's probably half right! He's expected to roast the bridegroom and to show no mercy. If he can do this without embarrassing the poor turkey in front of the opposition, he's a hero!

We'll be looking at these speeches in some detail a little farther on, but first, let's examine some important common factors.

The tribute

Any social speech should be looked upon as a tribute. The best man, for instance, even though his offering may be littered with insults, is still paying his friend a great compliment. He has taken the trouble of preparing a few special words and has gathered up the necessary courage to deliver his speech. This, surely, must rank as one of the most flattering wedding presents.

But *any* speech – social, political or corporate – can only ever be an exercise in superficiality. Think about it; you have only a very short time to get your points across, during which, hopefully, your audience will be glued to their seats. Come to think of it, with the right glue, it could work!

Your speech needs catchy words and humour, *but no real depth*. You have only about seven minutes and you simply can't go into detail. Social speech-making is not a medium that allows you the luxury of expanding and embellishing your thoughts. Give a speech too much substance and it becomes a lecture. People, nowadays, are programmed to absorb *soundbites*. These spoken headlines have to be linked together with little verbal bridges and need to follow a logical path. You'll see what I'm getting at later in the book, once you've looked at some examples. With this technique, however, one word in the wrong place and you've blown the joke. So a little farther on, I'll be showing you how to minimise that risk.

If I'm in the mood.

Putting it together

Before you start trawling the ocean of one-liners, it's important that you take a little time to learn what to do with your catch once it's landed.

Rhythm and style

A good speech, like a good song, needs a regular beat. It should have a rhythm of its own: peaks, troughs, crescendos and a climax. (Don't you love it when I talk dirty?)

Now, I can't start teaching you all that stuff in this little book, can I? Or *can* I?

By George, I think I can!

You see, if your material is structured properly, the rhythm of that speech, along with its highs and lows, happens almost automatically.

So let's not think too deeply about it. I'm going to recommend that your speech is a cleverly crafted succession of strong one-liners in a natural, flowing format.

That's it. No long jokes, no anecdotes, no stories … *one-liners*. (I should point out that I'm using the term 'one-liners' in a very generalised way; sometimes you'll be using two or three-line gags, sometimes the one-liner won't be a funny line at all – it could be a sentimental comment or piece of prose.)

In my opinion, the one-liner construction is ideal for wedding speeches; the rhythm is simple to maintain, your investment shows a return every seven or eight seconds and the format creates the illusion of a shorter, snappier speech – very handy if you're not exactly an experienced orator. If a joke or comment falls flat … so what? You're straight into the next line and, chances are, nobody will even notice that your one-liner didn't work.

On the other hand, the longer story or anecdote is an investment, which *has* to pay off. If a thirty-second story dies a death, you have a real problem.

We've all suffered the bloke who genuinely thinks he's a raconteur but in reality couldn't tell the difference between a comma and a coma!

There are occasions, however, when an incident or an amusing episode is so well known that you will be expected to make some mention of it. Don't repeat the whole story (unless you are Stephen Fry). As an experience, it may have been funny if you were there at the time, but as part of an otherwise fast-moving speech, you risk losing your audience. The trick is merely to allude to the event by using an appropriate one-liner.

For instance, let's assume many of the guests are aware that the bridegroom decided to cook for his fiancée one night and, as a result, both of them came down with food poisoning …

… just include the little-known fact that Dave attended the Karate School of Cookery … he was trained to kill with just one chop.

The bride's recent mishap with her new automobile could be acknowledged by saying: 'I wish people would stop going on about how she handles a car … for God's sake, if you don't like the way she drives, get off the pavement!'

The sad story of a chip pan fire could be covered by a mock telegram from the local chief fire officer.

Get the picture?

There's another very good reason to avoid anecdotes and reminiscences in wedding speeches; at a typical reception, half the guests probably won't know the other half. Do you really think that the bride's Auntie Phoebe genuinely gives a toss about how the best man and the bridegroom collaborated with the Manneken Pis to raise the water level of that fountain in Brussels during a football weekend? Can you honestly imagine the groom's workmates being enthralled at stories involving an eight-year-old girl's pink bootees and a cat?

The speech has to be entertaining, even to people who've never met the characters you're talking about. Your speech has to stand up by itself ... and by the way, so do you ... so don't get too canned until it's all over.

While you're waiting to speak, level with yourself ... are you slurring words? Are you liable to sway? ... or see double? ... or burp? ... or worse? If the answer to any of these questions is 'yeshh', don't be too alarmed; at least you've proved that the alcohol is working properly. However, as a speech-maker, you have a problem. You must switch immediately to water. I know, I know ... it's *horrible* stuff, and yes, I *do* realise what fishes do in it, but you've swallowed too much poison and water is the antidote.

Trust me; my brother-in-law's a *dentist*! (Mind you, that's all water under the bridge.)

Drink as much water as you can as fast as you can, whether you feel like it or not. Inevitably you'll suddenly find yourself doing a lot of travelling, but that's just nature's way of helping the water to circulate around your system. You should be straightened out within ten to fifteen minutes, but keep that water handy; you'll need it *during* your speech ... and here's why:

Note
Don't forget, once your speech is over, go straight back to alcohol ... after all, you don't want to make a habit of this water thing, do you? Just think ... if water can rot the soles of your shoes, imagine what it can do to your stomach!

Nerves have a really interesting effect upon an inexperienced speaker. Your mouth suddenly dries up. It feels like someone has stuffed a ball of blotting paper into it. As you try to speak, your tongue sticks to the roof of your mouth and you suddenly wish you had Teflon gums! It's a most peculiar phenomenon and one that requires a good supply of water most of the way through your speech.

But let us turn this into an advantage ...

Use the glass of water as a prop. It can have the same effect as the late George Burns's cigar: a punctuation device assisting in the control of your audience.

After you hit 'em with a one-liner, take a drink while they're laughing – don't worry, most of the material in this book is strong enough to give you enough time to have a gargle! – after a while, you'll find the crowd will begin to co-operate with you by stretching out their laughs until you've finished drinking. People really are *dumb* aren't they?

Making a speech for the first time is very much like making love for the first time. Because you may not have total confidence in what you're doing, the temptation is to rush it. She's going to change her mind … I'm going to lose it … we're going to be interrupted … oh.

You don't really know for sure whether your speech is going to be well received or not … Is the material funny enough? Is that one-liner in poor taste? Am I trying too hard?

Your audience will be slower to react at the beginning of your piece than at the end. Although you may know each one of them really well as individuals, together they have become an audience and you have become a speaker. As such you're new to each other. You need to reassess your relationship. You need to learn about them as an audience and they need to get the hang of you as a speaker.

Rushing into the next line too early is a sign that you are losing your nerve. Control it. As you deliver a line, wait just a little before you jump in with the next. Sometimes a gag will produce a delayed reaction and by the time the laughter builds up to its peak, you're halfway through the next line if you're not careful. So let the laughter run its course, and when it's just beginning to taper off, come in strong with the next gag.

You have to be sensible about this, of course. Don't stand up there in total silence; if a joke dies, bury it with the next.

By the time you're about halfway through the speech, you'll find that you are actually *conducting* the audience as you would an orchestra.

Don't feel guilty; they *love* being controlled. In show business, there's a technical name for people who really know how to manipulate their audiences … stars.

As you glance through the one-liners in this book, you may find that many of them need to be read aloud in order for you to see the joke. This illustrates how important it is to remember that you are writing for the *ear*, not for the *eye*.

Your audience will be *listening*, not *reading*. Your wording must sound natural; don't say 'she is' when you'd normally say 'she's' … don't say 'I am' when you'd normally say 'I'm' … don't say 'you will', say 'you'll' – unless, of course, you're deliberately *emphasising* the word 'will' as in 'You *will* tell your friends about this book, won't you?' Use normal language, not pseudo 'speech-talk'.

As my mother once advised her friend Celia, who was about to make an important speech: 'Don't try to be clever – just be yourself.'

Editing, padding and linking

The one-liner format makes it easy to edit on-site. Suppose someone you intended to welcome hasn't turned up; simply skip that part of the speech and carry on with the next segment. If, despite your personality and witty presentation, you begin to sense that the audience has had enough, it's an easy matter to cut from where you are to a later section, or even straight to the close of the speech.

With our one-liner construction, the omissions shouldn't affect the flow. Most of the lines are self-contained; if you're doing two or three one-liners about the bridegroom's attempts at keeping fit, just use the best one. Make sure, however, that your link words are suitable and are not too repetitive.

So now you're thinking, 'What the hell are *link words?*' Right? Yes, I *knew* what you were thinking … I told you we authors are very clever, didn't I?

Link words are what I call the little spoken punctuations and phrases used to move from one line or topic to another; words like 'Now …', 'Nevertheless …', 'You know …', 'Mind you …', 'After all …'.

Simply reciting pages of one-liners without the use of link words wouldn't work in a speech. You *need* them in order to bond your lines together, thereby creating the illusion of a natural progression.

Don't forget, you're coming out of a laugh into the next gag and it's more impressive for the audience to feel their laughter has forced you to pause than for you to appear as if you're throwing lines at them and hoping for the best.

You also need to 'bridge' from one subject to another in order to maintain a logical flow.

In the following example, I'm going to make three points about my victim:

1 He's lazy.

2 He's overweight.

3 He's a big drinker.

In other words, a perfectly normal average bloke.

I'll use link words to bond the jokes and bridging lines to progress through the subjects. The link words are in **bold**. The bridging lines are clearly indicated.

Here we go …

> Some people say Dave's lazy … this is most unfair;
> I know he had his window box paved over, but what does *that* prove?
> I prefer to call him a relaxoholic.
> **Of course**, he's heard that hard work never killed anyone …
> but he's taking no chances on being its first victim!
>
> **In fact**, he's stopped drinking coffee in the morning;
> it keeps him awake for the rest of the day!
> **Mind you**, he's not lazy when it comes to trying to keep himself fit …
>
> *(Bridging Line)*

He does a lot of jogging …
and you really have to take your hat off to him;
it's not easy to jog when you're eating a pizza!
Nevertheless, as you can see, he's in shape …
I mean, let's be fair; 'round' is a shape, isn't it?
Oh yes, Dave watches his weight …
well, he can't really miss it;
it's right out there in front of him!

You know, at home, he even has his own parallel bars …
One for brandy and one for scotch!

(Bridging Line)

O.K. … so Dave Newberry enjoys a drink …
what's wrong with that?
Most of the time he doesn't drink anything stronger than
pop.
Mind you, Pop will drink anything!
To be fair, he's cut down quite a bit;
this guy used to drink so much gin,
Gordon's thought he was a wholesaler!; etc. …

The above example illustrates how to use **link words**, not only for the purpose of joining lines together in a natural way, but also to keep your audience alert.

At times, it sounds as if you are defending the victim. However, this 'defence' is merely a device that gives you the excuse to continue laying into him.

Don't worry … he'll love it!

I think.

Note

In the various one-liners listed in this book, those suitable for bridging from one subject to the next will be indicated.

Don't be tempted to embellish a good line. If it ain't broke, don't fix it! One-liners usually contain a 'set-up' and a 'sting':

Set-up: I'd love to see her in something long and flowing …

Sting: … like a river!

The words 'long and flowing' are crucial. They conjure up the image of a beautiful ball-gown. The audience has been 'set up' for the surprise of the 'sting' line. Change these words and you lose the point. Put a line or even an extra word between 'flowing' and 'river' and you weaken the impact. Your audience has to retain the memory of the 'set-up' in order to realise they've been had.

Equally, if you feel you need to trim a one-liner, make sure that your cut doesn't damage the flow. Sometimes a gag can sound 'one-legged' if the rhythm is disturbed.

Think very carefully before messing about with one-liners. Be aware that certain words, which may appear innocuous or superfluous, could be part of the magic that makes us laugh. Removing those words may be fatal to the line.

Some words are simply *funny* words. For example:

'Hen'	–	nothing	'Chicken'	–	funny
'Gloves'	–	nothing	'Socks'	–	funny
'Beige'	–	nothing	'Puce'	–	funny.

The expression 'Father-in-law' is not in the least funny, whereas 'Mother-in-law' is absolutely *sidesplitting* … at least it would be if it wasn't so tragic!

I should point out at this juncture that I've always tried to avoid analysing comedy; it's a bit like love – if you have to define it, you don't deserve it. A line is either humorous, or it isn't. However, sometimes an illustration or two may help someone avoid ruining an otherwise funny line, so I apologise – it's a dirty job, but somebody's got to do it!

Notes, memory or script

Many experts advise against writing out your speech in full. They feel that this method would make your performance sound false and contrived. I happen to differ. It ain't necessarily so. Let's look at the alternatives.

Cue cards

To start with, I think these things are distracting and look very silly. They give the impression that you've hastily jotted down a few words on some odd place cards you found a few minutes ago in the cloak-room.

A five-minute speech could contain about fifty cues. At the normal delivery speed, your card-shuffling will very rapidly begin to fascinate the audience more than whatever you are saying.

Notes on a sheet of paper

Not too bad a method for some speeches or presentations, but remember – the one-liner format in particular requires precise construction. All sorts of things can go wrong if your notes don't trigger the correct wording.

Consider this …

> We're here to celebrate a love match, pure and simple;
> Lucy's pure and David's … a very nice guy!

Good line. Guaranteed to get a laugh. But what if your notes said 'LOVE MATCH' and you delivered it like this …

> We're here to celebrate a love match, plain and simple;
> Lucy's plain and … Oh shit!

To be safe, your notes should have read: 'CELEBRATE – LOVE MATCH – PURE & SIMPLE'.

Hardly worth the bother is it? You might as well write it out in full.

Learn it by heart

Unless you have a photographic memory, a wealth of experience and nerves of steel, forget it! Because chances are, you will! You're going to be nervous in any case; even the most seasoned professional expects a few butterflies before he stands up. Why inflict upon yourself the added terror of forgetting your words? Believe me, when you stand up to speak, you're going to need as much confidence as you can falsify.

Instead of trying to memorise a fast-moving speech of this kind, you'd do better to utilise some of my sneakier techniques. These little tricks were designed to make the audience almost unaware that you're reading the whole thing. What's more, they work. So instead of sitting up night after night, attempting to learn 1,400 crucial words, use just a fraction of that time and effort to develop the knack of presenting your speech in a natural and relaxed manner.

Here's what I recommend:

Write the speech out in full on reasonably heavy paper, about 17 x 24 cm (7 x 9 in). The paper shouldn't be too flimsy; the pages need to be easy to separate as you are reading.

Use felt-tip pens in varying colours; for instance, one joke or small paragraph in blue, the next in black. The following line could be in green, followed by purple, and so on.

Finally, underline certain key words in red. These could be words you need to emphasise, or merely the 'bones' of a line that could be glanced at and used as shorthand.

I'm sure you've seen speech-makers happily reading from typewritten or handwritten sheets of A4. Realising, quite rightly, that they need to look away from their script and make some eye contact with their audience from time to time, they look up and finish a line or two from memory as they glance around the room.

Then they look down again ...

Silence ... *more* silence ... **excruciating** silence.

A desperate and embarrassing search has begun. The poor sap has lost his place!

'Where was I? Up the top? No, I've done that bit. Somewhere about three-quarters of the way down, I think … er …'

Trouble is, all the words on the page look exactly the same. It's just one sheet of writing.

However, with my recommended system of using coloured text, it's much less likely that you'll lose your place.

Don't be concerned, you don't need to memorise the colour you were on before you looked away from your script; for some reason your subconscious takes care of all that. It usually leads you back to the correct place.

Practise it … even if it doesn't work for you one hundred percent, at least you'll be able to scan the page at a faster rate. Remember, you only have to look at the beginning of each topic to know whether it's the right one or not, and you ought only to have about eight to ten one-liners per page.

As I said at the beginning of the chapter on editing, the one-liner construction makes it much easier to cut whole sections of your speech in 'real-time' if necessary. The coloured text system makes it easier still.

A very sneaky ploy

Here's a little trick to make people unaware that, in fact, you're reading your speech word for word …

Start off with a couple of announcements – it's perfectly natural for you to be reading these – then you can go straight into your speech, still reading … and they won't even notice.

This trick is ideal for the best man who, in any case, will be expected to read some telegrams. However, there's nothing to stop the bride's father or the groom opening something like this:

Ladies and gentlemen,
before I start, I've been asked to make the following announcements;

Will the owner of toupee, serial number 727318 kindly collect it from the foyer …
it's beginning to confuse the cat!

I have good news and bad news …
first the good news …
After the speeches, the bride's uncle Stanley will be giving us all a song …
That was the good news …
and that'll give you some idea of how bad the *bad* news is!

By the way, Stanley will be singing that lovely standard, 'I'm dancing tonight with tears in my eyes, 'cos the girl in my arms is a boy'.

Ladies and gentlemen,
we're all here today because …

… and you're into the speech.

People are now quite used to seeing you glancing down at the paper, and, as long as you bring your head up and look around the room regularly as you speak, they won't be conscious of you reading from a script.

By the way, during your speech, always make sure your next page is ready for you well before you come to the end of your current page.

Hello Mike!

You'll be reading from a full script, so you'll need both hands available throughout your speech. One hand will be holding the paper, the other will need to be free for page-turning, gestures, water-sipping, toasting or – should you insult the wrong guy – *self-defence*.

It's almost essential, therefore, to ensure that you have a free-standing microphone. I prefer a table-stand, but any mike-stand will do. You'll have to arrange for this in advance. Don't trust it to luck and *don't* believe people who tell you to leave it all to them ... it's *your* responsibility ... *you are* the one who'll look awkward if things are not right.

Don't test the mike by blowing on it or saying; 'One, two, one, two!' ... if you do, I'll come over there and knock your bloody block off *myself!* Right?

Just tap the mike gently to make sure it's working. If it's not, get someone to switch it on.

Speak from the table if you can, not from the stage. The stage becomes a barrier between you and the audience, and interferes with that special, intimate relationship. Instead of speaking as part of the crowd, the platform or dance floor makes it a case of 'us and them' and you won't get the results your material deserves.

When you speak, speak loudly, speak clearly and speak with confidence. After all, you can afford to speak with confidence when your material is strong, and it *will be* ... stick around.

 Material

Try to use totally original gags; it doesn't matter where you steal them from. After all, the line between 'inspired by' and 'nicked from' is a very fine one.

As you will have gathered from the originality demonstrated in this book, I don't need to nick anything. When I do, it's for the pure joy of larceny. However, as I invented so much of this material myself, I have a request – if one day, you happen to find that we're both speaking at the same function, please exercise some professional etiquette; steal from some other bugger's book instead.

You get extra points with an audience if your material is, or sounds, original. If you personalise your one-liners accurately enough, you may well create that illusion. You also get extra points for topicality. What's the big news story on the day of the wedding? Can you adapt a line cleverly enough to refer to it?

No?

Oh.

Tough!

How to use 'roast' lines and insults

The important thing to remember about 'roast' material is that it has to have a ring of truth about it in order to be funny. These jokes are verbal caricatures. They take a defect or a quirk and exaggerate it. If the bridegroom is a little – how can I put it? – careful with money, the best man may well say:

> Some men marry for love,
> some men marry for companionship …
> Dave needed a new toaster!

If the bride recently had an accident in the kitchen and called it 'dinner', her father may have to admit that he's going to miss her cooking ... as often as he can! Even the thought of her mashed potatoes gives him a lump in his throat!

However, if the bridegroom is known to be extravagant and the bride is a cordon bleu cook, the lines are meaningless.

Whatever you do, don't contrive a situation or a characteristic in order to justify using a one-liner, no matter how funny you think it is. Try to hit the button, but don't be *too* cruel. Even if the roastee is liable to take it well, many members of the audience are going to be concerned for your victim's feelings if you cross that sensitive line.

Think about the person you wish to rib; you may find something in his (never *her*) appearance – shortish, balding, beer belly? Is he a lousy golfer? A lazy bugger? A wimp? I hope so. All that makes for a much better speech.

Good taste

These days, a wedding speech needn't be 'squeaky clean', but you must use some common sense. Learn the art of stopping before offence ... just like that good-for-nothing horse I used to own.

Select every one-liner with great care – especially the ones in this book. If in doubt; leave it out. (Poetry's a piece of cake, isn't it?)

Know your customers. Judge how broadminded the crowd is liable to be. Will members of the clergy be present? Is there a strait-laced maiden aunt around? It wouldn't hurt to check things out.

I discussed this whole question with the Right Reverend Noel Jones, Bishop of Sodor and Man. He feels that members of the clergy are not your problem; these days, churchmen are much more broadminded than people give them credit for. Beware, however, of certain guests ... the old colonel uncle, the ancient aunt ... a wedding is, after all, a *family* occasion, with guests ranging from grandmothers to young tearaways through to little children. 'It's best', said the Bishop, 'to tread the middle path of safety. You'll almost certainly get away with near-the-mark references to the forthcoming honeymoon, complete with all the sexual innuendoes. This is expected and nobody is going to be too shocked.' As an example, he quoted the old evergreen: 'The bride and groom won't be long, they're upstairs, putting their things together.' However, Bishop Jones felt that 'deep vulgarity' is unnecessary and will probably offend. 'Bear in mind', he said, 'that at a wedding, many members of the two families are meeting for the first time. What you say in your speech may well play a part in the opinion formed by one family towards the other.'

I'm grateful to the Bishop for his advice and guidance on the subject; it's valuable to have his opinion as one of Britain's religious leaders.

Nowadays, as I've shown, you *can* get away with fairly risqué material, but never be too vulgar; avoid being 'lavatorial' and try to be subtle with sexual references.

For normal wedding receptions, the serious four-letter words are definitely taboo, of course. However, provided you use them only occasionally and advisedly, words like 'pissed', 'bullshit', 'crap' are usually all right in the correct context. (Out of context they'll sound as stark as they did in the previous sentence, so watch it!)

Over the years, as a speech-writer and speech-maker, I've learned that a well-written humorous speech that manages to avoid vulgarity will win you respect from an audience. This will enhance your image and up your reputation. Nearly every client of mine has upped *his* reputation ... **up yours**!

Clichés

I'm tempted to say 'avoid clichés like the plague!' but that would be a cheap and facile gag and, therefore, perfectly suitable for this book.

The real difficulty with clichés is that, by their very nature, they have become so much a part of the language it's easy to forget they're being used, so at least try to be conscious of them.

Of course, to be fair on these hackneyed phrases, they wouldn't have *become* clichés had they not been expressive and appropriate in the first place. However, their original meanings have often become obscured and, worse – people get them wrong.

You've heard the expression 'laughing all the way to the bank!' Well, you shouldn't have done! The correct phrase is '*crying* all the way to the bank!' So there!

The line seems to have been invented by Liberace and used in his autobiography. He wrote: 'When the reviews are bad, I tell my staff that they can join me as I cry all the way to the bank.'

To fill a speech or even a conversation with trite banalities and stereotypical phrases merely drives people into the clutches of professional writers like me. So keep it up.

 # Content and style

It's time for the first of our one-liners ...

Openers

A few ideas designed to grab an early giggle.

Family and friends ...

I *would* call you 'Ladies and gentlemen', but I happen to know better.

Ladies and gentlemen,

it's been such an exciting day that I'm absolutely speechless ...

which is probably very good news for most of you.

Ladies and gentlemen,

before I begin, Marks and Spencer have asked me to announce that this ...

is a Co-op suit.

Ladies and gentlemen,

let me first of all apologise if my speech seems a little rushed ...

I have to speak fast 'cos, frankly, my material sucks!

Ladies and gentlemen,

what I have to say today may well bring a smile to your throat and a lump to your lips.

Ladies and gentlemen,

I'm very relieved it's my turn to speak at last ...

the valium's beginning to wear off.

Ladies and gentlemen,
I've been asked to say a few words, so here goes …
cornstarch … oxyacetylene … onomatopoeia …
and now for the speech …

Ladies and gentlemen,
I'm so happy and excited, I can hardly wait to hear what
I've got to say.

Ladies and gentlemen,
This is my A.B.C.D. speech …
above and beyond the call of duty.

Ladies and gentlemen,
this is the moment you've all been waiting for …
and there it goes!

Ladies and gentlemen,
I'm delighted to have been asked to make this speech
today …
I've been dying to get out of that bloody house.

Ladies and gentlemen,
I'm only going to speak for a couple of minutes because
of my throat …
if I go on too long, Elayne has threatened to cut it.

Family and friends …
I'd like to admit straight away that I was a little nervous
earlier on, but happily I'm feeling much better …
I'm completely at my ease now because, after all, I
realise I'm in front of my own kind of people …
drunks!

(You may substitute 'piss artistes' if you feel you can get away with it;
it'll get a bigger laugh.)

Father of the bride

STOP!

IF YOU HAVE JUST ARRIVED DIRECT FROM PAGE NINE,

BEFORE ATTEMPTING TO READ THIS CHAPTER,

DO YOURSELF A FAVOUR – RETURN TO PAGE ELEVEN.

In any speech, it can be quite difficult to maintain the balance between being a gushing, sentimental old softie and a cold fish. This tends to be more of a problem when it comes to the speech made by the father of the bride. He needs to let his guests and family know how much he cares for his little darling, yet, if he uses the sincere language of a loving father, his audience is liable to start throwing up en masse.

You see, sincerity is not enough.

I know many *genuine* people who just can't help sounding like phonies; it's the language they use and the tone they adopt. To alleviate the 'O.T.T.' effect, avoid being too nice for too long. Alternate your sincere observations with little bits of humour. I call this style 'ping-pong'.

Here's a format that should give you an idea of what I'm getting at. This is not exactly a speech, these lines are the building blocks; you will need to add a few more words of thanks (don't forget the bride's mother), select some more one-liners and link them together to maintain the 'ping-pong' effect.

> Bride and bridegroom, family and friends,
> ladies and gentlemen,
> this won't be a long speech;
> I don't have that large a vocabulary.
>
> I'd like to thank you all for coming …
> especially those of you who knew I'd be saying a few
> words but turned up nevertheless.

Some of you have travelled considerable distances in order to share this happy day with us ...

we have guests here from all over the world;
New Zealand, Mombassa, Manitoba ...

these are the only three places not represented here this afternoon.

So we greet you all with added pleasure and our sincere appreciation for the trouble you've taken to be here ...

for you, drinks are half price!

Ladies and gentlemen,

there's something very special about a wedding that we often overlook ...

it's a unique opportunity for two families and friends of those families to start getting to know each other.

Of course, sometimes that's asking for trouble ...
but in this case I must say, I don't think we'll have any problems ...

Our two families now have a common bond and I'm delighted to be sharing the day with Janice and Allen – my daughter's new in-laws.

I also look forward to sharing with them, the future pleasures that will, no doubt, come to us through Lucy and Dave.

It's inevitable, I suppose, that a day like today inspires a few memories ...

in particular, memories of this young bride's formative years.

You know, when Lucille was born, she looked exactly like me ...

then they turned her the right way up and all was well.

People think of my daughter as a very bright young lady, and so she is …

but we weren't too sure when she was younger …

at kindergarten, Lucy was different from all the other five year olds …

she was eleven!

And I have to admit that even at Victoria College she was not the brightest of pupils …

One day in the assembly hall she saw a sign saying 'WET FLOOR' …

so she *did*!

At one stage, I had my doubts about the crowd she was hanging around with …

I used to have to pay her pocket money in unmarked bills!

But our Lucy was never any trouble at home. She was a quiet girl. Every now and then, I'd glance up at the shelf and there she'd be …

waiting …

Thankfully, today marks the end of that waiting and I know that Lucy feels that Dave has been well worth waiting for. He is, after all, a fine young man with many interests … he's into sailing and golf and, so far, his progress in the world of business has been meteoric. I'm confident that my daughter is in good hands. After all, show me a man with both feet on the ground, and I'll show you a man who …

can't put his trousers on!

Dave, you certainly know how to make Lucy happy and I'm quite sure you'll continue to do so.

Welcome to the family …

and believe me, you *are* welcome to the bloody family!

I think you'll find that Lucy is going to be an asset to you in all sorts of ways ...

She's quite a career girl herself and, even though a father shouldn't really say it, Lucille has everything it takes to be a success in business ...

a quiet charm, a persuasive manner, the ability to grovel without laddering her tights ...

But Elayne and I are very proud parents today ...

I'm sure you'll all agree that Lucy looks absolutely stunning this afternoon ...

and the nice thing is, she's as lovely on the inside as she is on the outside ...

(Pause for 'hear hears')

Lucy and Dave ...

marriage is a great university. It teaches you patience, consideration, understanding ...

and all sorts of crap you wouldn't even need if you stayed *single*!

I'm totally confident that the two of you will graduate with honours.

Ladies and gentlemen,

please join us in drinking a toast to the happy couple, Lucy and Dave ...

I know you're going to be great together ...

God bless you and good luck to you both!

(Raise glass)

See what I mean? First sweet, then zap! First this way, then that. Ping-pong.

By the way, another good thing about the ping-pong method is that the audience doesn't want to miss the next one-liner, so they actually concentrate ... in much the same way as you can't put this book down because I'm so bloody hilarious!

Extra lines suitable for the father of the bride

In addition to 'roast' lines and other zingers elsewhere in this book, the following may be specifically useful.

My function today is simple; to give away the bride.

Of course, after paying for all this lot, the bride is all I have left *to* give away!

(Bridging line)

I'll never forget the thrill of watching our little Lucy as she took those momentous, unsteady, faltering steps.
She was sixteen years old and totally pissed!

She ran away from home once, but for three days nobody missed her ...
we all thought she was still in the bathroom!

She was always a good girl ...
in fact she's got so used to saying 'no', she nearly screwed up the wedding ceremony!

I'm going to miss her, but let's face it, she's not getting married one day too soon ... they've been together for eight years.

Eight years! Come to think of it, instead of the Wedding March I should have got the organist to play the Hallelujah Chorus!

This morning, my sin-in-law became my son-in-law.

Living together without being married is like being punished for a crime you didn't commit!

When Dave first approached me and said: 'I've come to ask for your daughter's hand' …
I told him: 'It's all right with me, as long as you take the one that's always in my pocket!'.
'No', he said, 'you don't understand …
I want your daughter for my wife!'
I said: 'What would your *wife* do with her?'

I've come to think of Dave as I do my own son …
the one I threw out of the house and disowned.

My daughter really likes the good things in life …
I don't know if you overheard this, but earlier, when the vicar asked if there were any objections, Lucy said: 'Yeah! What's all that crap about "for richer or for poorer?"!'

I was so proud to see her today as she swept down the aisle …
Believe me, mate, that's the last time you're ever going to see *her* sweep!

(Bridging line)

Elayne and I really hope that Lucy and Dave are going to make grandparents of us.
Of course it's their decision, but I must say that people with no children are missing out …
they'll never know what a thrill it is to come home after a hard day, sit down to a hot dinner and watch someone stuffing spaghetti hoops up their nose!

Kids are crucial to family life …
without them, how the hell would we ever be able to programme a video recorder?!

Lucy and Dave are marrying in their early twenties
because they want their children young. Quite right.

After all, who wants old children?

You may wish to incorporate into your speech, a quotation on the
subject of marriage. Don't use more than one or two. You'll find some
near the end of this book.

Father's advice to the bride and bridegroom

As the two of you go forward hand in hand into the big,
wide world ...

I can do no better than to offer you some of the advice
that has been passed down in our family from
generation to generation ...

and never used.

There are three things you must remember to give during
a marriage: inspiration, income, in.

The best way to make sure you always remember your
wedding anniversary is to forget it just once.

Make it a point never to argue about anything not worth
arguing about.

But be careful; sometimes you can get into a fight trying
to decide what's worth arguing about!

Live each day as if it were your last, and each night as if it
were your first.

Let your bride know who's boss right from the start ...
there's no point trying to fool yourself!

Take my wife ... please!

If – and *only* if – the new mother-in-law is a good sport, these lines are for the new father-in-law ...

Elayne and I have been married *twenty-seven years* ...
honestly, it seems like yesterday ...
and you know what a lousy day yesterday was!

Speaking for myself, I simply couldn't imagine being single again ...
at least not without getting a silly grin on my face!

In all that time, neither of us has even *considered* divorce ...
Homicide, but never divorce.

But I just *love* being married ...
especially those quiet times apart!

As you know, a 25th wedding anniversary is Silver ...
A 50th anniversary is Gold.
Our next anniversary is ...
Shrapnel!

Since we were married, I never looked at another woman;
she put me right off 'em!

I never kept any secrets from my wife ...
I tried, but I never could.

On our tenth anniversary, we revisited the hotel we went to for our honeymoon ...
This time, *I* ran into the bathroom and cried!

You know, Elayne believes that I'm the world's greatest lover …
but she's never quite managed to catch me at it!

We've shared the same bed for twenty-seven years …
She sleeps in it at night – I take the day shift.

I've been very depressed lately;
my wife has been threatening to leave me …
even *that* hasn't cheered me up!

I never knew what true happiness was until I got married and then …
it was too bloody late!

We have a sign at home:
'Views expressed by husbands are not necessarily those of the management.'

I saw a girl in 'Playboy' who measured 39–24–35 and I finally figured out what's wrong with my wife
she's inside out!

The cook

The following lines are, on the face of it, directed at females. Most of them may easily be adapted to knock the male cook. I'm not being sexist, honest.

Anyway, what if I am?

I hate to say it, but she's not a very good cook …
we had people over for dinner two weeks ago and they're still sitting there!

She used to dress to kill …
now she just cooks that way.

Her cooking leaves a little to be desired …
namely – taste!

There are two reasons why husbands leave home:
wives who *can* cook and won't,
and wives who *can't* cook and do.

For the last six weeks she served up chicken every
Thursday …
What do you mean 'What's wrong with that?'
It was the same chicken!

She's such a bad cook,
she won't lick her own fingers!

I had a feeling there was something wrong from day one
when I got up, walked into the kitchen and found her
ironing the bacon!

The recipe called for a little flour,
so she threw in a tulip.

I came home once to find she'd left me a note:
'Dinner's in the cookery book, page 14.'

When the dish ran away with the spoon, they were
escaping from her kitchen.

You've got to give her some credit for being inventive …
Who else would have come up with 'Soup in a Basket'?

My job, when she's about to start cooking, is to go from
room to room, removing batteries from the smoke
alarms.

I remember the day she baked a coconut pie …
how she got the pie into that coconut, I've *no* idea!

Most days there'd be a line of pygmies outside the
kitchen window, queuing up to dip their arrows in her
soup.

Lately she's been cooking so much fish,
I've starting breathing through my cheeks!

Her specialities include:
'Avocado You'll Regret', 'Smoked Salmonella', 'Boeuf
Beenangorne' and 'Hash Black Potatoes'.

She spends all her time in the kitchen.
She's always baking, baking, baking …
now that wouldn't be so bad, but – salads?

People are always asking her for her recipes …
I suppose they're hoping she'll give away her only copy.

She specialises in Cajun cookery …
every morning she makes blackened toast.

The bridegroom

STOP!

IF YOU HAVE JUST ARRIVED DIRECT FROM PAGE NINE,

BEFORE ATTEMPTING TO READ THIS CHAPTER,

DO YOURSELF A FAVOUR – RETURN TO PAGE ELEVEN.

In my opinion, the bridegroom's speech – for all the reasons I gave earlier – is the most difficult to pitch exactly right. He'll be speaking in front of his new in-laws and their guests, his bride (probably still somewhat bonded to Mummy and Daddy), his own family and his leering, drunken, mickey-taking friends.

What's called for is a clever balancing trick.

Let me refer you to the 'ping-pong' technique I wrote about at the beginning and end of the previous section devoted to the father of the bride. The groom may find this cheap trick equally useful.

In his speech, the bridegroom – speaking also on behalf of his bride – should begin by responding to the toast made by his new father-in-law. He may wish to thank his in-laws for their hospitality (if applicable), and his own parents for all their help and support over the years.

At this point, his eyes begin to fill with tears as he tells everyone how lucky he is to have found his bride. (I suggest a little raw onion hidden behind the nail of the index finger.)

He thanks all his friends and family for coming along, shows gratitude for the generous wedding gifts, compliments the ushers on doing a fine job, mentions how beautiful the bridesmaids are (by the way, be careful; it's not easy to hold a champagne glass with your fingers crossed) and winds up by proposing a toast to them.

All very nice, but where's the bite?

One thing's for certain, when the best man starts to speak, the bridegroom is really going to have to put up with some put-downs.

My advice is ATTACK!

Go for a pre-emptive strike.

Bring the best man into your speech, thank him for all he's done to help make the day a success, then … pluck his feathers out one by one!

Like the sample text I used for the bride's father, the following sequence is not exactly a speech, these lines are merely the building blocks; you will need to personalise them and to expand them as necessary.

When insulting the best man, think of his weaknesses and his peculiarities and choose some appropriate lines. Don't forget, these are spoken caricatures … just exaggerate the truth.

If there are no bridesmaids involved, it may be nice to close the speech with a toast to your new bride. Choose one from the 'Toasts' section.

> Host and hostess, family and friends, ladies and gentlemen:
>
> Today you are looking at a very happy man …
> and I wish you'd turn round and look at me instead, because I'm trying to make a speech!
>
> Firstly, I'd like to thank my new father-in-law, Jack Lucas, for his kind words.
> It's amazing what some people will say when they're not under oath.
>
> Of course, this is a very important day for me – second only to my stag night – so I'm sure you'll understand if I seem to be a little nervous … it's only natural …
> marriage is, after all, a pretty big step … and these days, you've got to be careful what you step *into*!
>
> I must say we've had some very nice wedding presents and Lucy joins me in thanking you for your generosity …
> as a matter of fact, we're beginning to regret that we didn't have an engagement party.

But of course, the 'presents' that we're really thrilled about ... is your *presence* here on this very special day.

It's wonderful to see you all.

Thank you Jack and Elayne, not only for your superb hospitality this evening and for your many kindnesses, but also for giving me your beautiful daughter.

I promise I'll take good care of her and I'll always try to make her happy.

Like Lucy, I was lucky enough to be brought up in an enlightened, well-balanced and loving atmosphere by two terrific parents.

My Mum and Dad are remarkable people ... they taught me so much and gave me solid-gold advice, leadership and love.

You know, Dad was always a wonderful provider and a hard-working man ... he used to get up at 5.30am to do nineteen hours of strenuous work and thought nothing of it! ...

as it happens, I'm very much the same ...

I don't think much of it either!

I'm delighted that Mum and Dad are with us today, helping us both to enjoy the happiness of this occasion. It gives me an opportunity, publicly, to thank them for everything they've done in guiding and shaping my life.

Thank you, Mum and Dad.

You know, I married this young lady because, quite frankly, only the best will do for Newberry.

You see, I've always been very fussy ...

At one time, I was looking for a girl who didn't smoke, didn't drink, wasn't interested in The Chippendales and didn't keep asking for money for clothes ...

When I finally found one, she was *nine*!

Now, don't get me wrong …
I've had my wild moments …
There was a time in my early twenties when I really
began living the life of Riley …
Then one day, Riley came home earlier than usual and I
had to make a run for it!

But a man can't carry on like that forever …
for medical reasons more than anything else.
In any case, society *resents* that much happiness.

Well, **poo** to society 'cos I found something a lot better,
and today my Lucy promised to devote herself to loving
me until the end of time …
Or 'Newsweek', whichever subscription expires first!

Of course, this is a girl with many wonderful qualities …
anyone who knows her will understand why I consider
myself a very lucky man today.
Mind you, her time-keeping leaves a lot to be desired …
She's *always* late …
In fact, British Airways have just named a delayed flight
in her honour!

I would like to say, however, that she's really excellent
around the home …
I really *would* like to say that …
Wish I could.
You know, Lucy was trying to bake a cake recently and
the recipe said: 'Separate two eggs' …
so she put one in the living room and one the hall!
She'll catch on.

But I really couldn't ask for a better woman …
if I did, she'd kill me!
Mind you, after this speech, she's probably going to kill
me anyway!

In case some of you were wondering, let me put your minds at rest …

there's no possible way I was going to forget to mention the four brave survivors from my stag party …

Thank you Richard, Keith and John for acting as ushers this morning …

and for getting it right! …

I'm impressed.

As for Andy, besides being my brother, he's also my greatest friend and I'm proud to have him as best man …

not that he's going to get the chance to prove *that* tonight!

Funnily enough, last spring, Andy went to a nudist wedding in the South of France, and – d'you know what? – he came within one inch of being best man there as well.

At one point he turned to a bridesmaid and said, 'Don't look now, but I think I'm falling in love with you.'

You know, they say that blood is thicker than water …

Andy Newberry is thicker than both.

It really is impossible to praise this guy too highly …

it's impossible to praise him at all …

he's *crap*!

And yet, ladies and gentlemen, as you get to know him, Andy will begin to have an effect on you …

He'll creep into your heart …

He'll creep into your mind …

He'll creep into your soul …

He's the biggest creep in town!

But he's *our* creep!

By the way, Channel Four is planning a documentary on his sex life …
it's called 'Sixty Seconds'.

He'll be getting up to speak in a moment or two, and he has some really unusual material today …
his suit!
So I suppose I'd better make way now and give him a chance.

Ladies and gentlemen,
this is the happiest day of my entire life, and I really must thank Lucy for pointing that out to me.

We've had a really wonderful day …
starting at St Matthew's and continuing here with a delicious meal …
By the way, my compliments to the microwave.

Thank you all for giving us so much pleasure by sharing our wedding day with us.
Now, will you please join me in drinking the traditional toast to our gorgeous bridesmaids – Laura, Trudy and Angela …
and to Christopher, our macho pageboy.
Good luck and thank you for everything.
Cheers

(Raise glass.)

Extra lines suitable for the bridegroom

In addition to 'roast' lines and other zingers elsewhere in this book, the following may be specifically useful.

I had to work very hard on this speech; it's too easy to make embarrassing mistakes …
like the one my friend Simon made when he thanked his in-laws for giving him a perky copulator!

When I went to my boss and asked him for a raise, at first he turned me down.
He said: 'I know you can't get married on what I pay you and some day you'll thank me!'

My boss asked me how much time off I'd like for the honeymoon …
I said: 'Very nice of you, what do you suggest?'
He said: 'I don't know, I haven't seen the bride.'

You know, I was in a position to marry anyone I pleased …
Unfortunately, I didn't seem to please anyone.

You know, the first time I set eyes on Lucy, I was immediately struck by her looks …
to me, she was 'drop-dead gorgeous!' …
I said: 'You're gorgeous!'
She said: 'Drop dead!'

From the very beginning she had me eating out of her hand;
it certainly saved a lot of washing up!

When I first started going out with Lucy, it was only natural
that I should take her home to meet my parents …

of course, they liked Lucy immediately – they took to her
straight away …

trouble was, they didn't approve of *me*!

Andy is a very talented man,

very talented indeed …

He's a gifted designer, a shrewd entrepreneur, a witty
raconteur, a deep thinker and a sensitive, caring one-
woman man.

Andy is so talented, he can *fake* all of that!

You know, in life we sometimes take things for granted.

For instance, I never realised just how much I owed to
my father …

until he foreclosed on my house.

You may wish to incorporate into your speech, a quotation on the
subject of marriage. Don't use more than one or two. You'll find some
near the end of this book.

The one-liners continue …

Balding

Andy suffers from a receding hairline – it's receded all
the way down to his arse!

He used to have nice wavy hair,

but then one day, it waved 'bye bye' …

it was a sad parting.

His hair has turned prematurely gone.

He's thinking of going to Africa …

to find his roots.

It's great to see Andy having some fun and letting his hair down.
It's only fair – after all, his hair let *him* down.

This guy is living proof that it's not only tough at the top, it's shiny too.

He keeps his hat on with a suction cap.

If there were such a thing as a hair fairy,
he'd be a wealthy man today.

He used to have a crew cut, but the crew bailed out.

When Andy hit adolescence, he shot up so fast he went straight through his hair.

Andy … good news. There's a wonderful new treatment for baldness on the market;
it doesn't grow hair …
it shrinks your head to fit what hair you have left!

The church and the dreaded clergy

The church:
The first time you go, they throw water on you …
The second time you go, they throw rice on you …
The third time you go, they throw earth on you …

I asked the vicar if he believed in sex before the wedding.
He said: 'Not if it delays the ceremony.'

By the way, the vicar has asked me to point out that
his church accepts all denominations …
fivers, tenners, fifties.

Did you notice, he's put up a sign outside the church:
'Keep off the grass.
This means *thou*!'

Of course there's life after death;
you don't think we get off *that* easily do you?

The story of Adam and Eve makes you think, doesn't it?
Adam didn't have a mother-in-law …
and he lived in paradise.

Here's a man who followed the Ten Commandments all
his life …
Never caught *up* with any of them, but …

In the words of J. C. Crawford –
the naughty vicar of Branfield –
'Well what did you expect?
I *am* a missionary!'

Silly stuff

This is just a smattering of daft bits and pieces. Who knows? One of them may just fit the bill.

She tried to kill him with a look, but she was cross-eyed,
so she killed another man.

He once joined a girl to forget the Foreign Legion.

She couldn't make it today;
she's got a part-time job at the stables
and her work is piling up.

He used to wake himself up with his snoring.
Not any more …
now he sleeps in another room!

He looked very distinguished standing there with a pipe
in his mouth …
but then he started blowing bubbles.

He's a very strange guy;
I saw him last week, walking his goose!

This is a man who doesn't know what he wants …
and is willing to go through *hell* … to get it!

When he was a kid, his mother used to say:
'Stop biting your nails! …
or at least, put your shoes back on when you've finished!'

I couldn't find any alphabet soup at Tesco's on
Saturday …
It must be out of print.

The first time he saw her swimming in the sea
he thought she was a girl worth wading for.

She's always on some kind of diet.
There was one where she could only eat waxed fruit …
One night, she broke into Madame Tussaud's and binged
on Julian Clary!

At one point in his life, he fell in love with a lady painter
and decorator and was overcome with emulsion.

He very nearly had a telepathic girlfriend once …
but she left him before they even met.

I'll never forget the first time I saw this character …
He was standing in the canteen all bleary eyed, coffee in
hand.
No cup, just coffee in his hand.

After he saw the film 'Roots', he tried tracing his family …
but they refused to lie down on the paper.

Two satellite dishes met on a roof, fell in love and got
married.
The ceremony wasn't much, but the reception was
brilliant.

Ladies and gentlemen,
yesterday I had a spell of déjà vu …
Or am I having it now?

Thick

He willed his brain to medical science.
Five years ago they came and picked it up.

They say a fool and his money are soon parted …
I first met him when he was out looking for his money.

I remember the time he discovered his tree of
knowledge …
It was a bonsai.

Here's a man who laughs at adversity …
especially if you ask him to spell it.

He saw a car parked outside his house with a sign in the
window saying 'neighbourhood watch'.
He kept tapping on the windscreen asking what time it
was.

He's always been thick;
when his mother was pregnant with him, she was
arrested for being a dope carrier.

This is a man who believes that marshmallows are brain
food …
In his case, he's right.

When he used to go hitch-hiking,
he always set out early to avoid the traffic.

If you ask me,
I think he had his ears pierced too deep.

His brain scan read: 'out to lunch'.

His heart is in the right place …
It's just his mind we can't find.

It would be quite wrong to call him an idiot …
he can clothe himself and perform simple tasks, so
technically; he's a moron.

(See also 'Naïve' and 'Put-downs'.)

The womaniser

Some of these lines are aimed at bachelors, some at married guys with
eyes. Don't roast the married ones on this subject in front of their
wives.

Trust me on this.

All women look alike to him …
fanciable!

He's had so much on the side,
he walks with a limp.

He loved her for her mind …
until he found out that sex was the farthest thing from it!

He once got kicked in the face just for kissing the
bride …
Mind you, it was two years after the ceremony.

The first time I ever met him, he had a beautiful woman
on his arm …
best tattoo I ever saw.

He met his wife in a singles bar …
Both of them were surprised.

As a lover … well, suffice it to say
the girls call him 'Superman' …
He's faster than a speeding bullet!

There was one special girl I remember …
She really had something that hit him between the
eyes …
a husband.

They used to teach the birds and bees about *him*!

Fussy? He'll go for anything with a shadow!

He believes in wine, women and so-long.

He's beginning to think it's time for him to take a wife.
The only question is: whose?

He didn't say he was taking her to Florida,
he said he was going to Tampa with her!

Definitions

Baby   A bald head and a pair of lungs.

Bachelor   A selfish, callous undeserving man who has cheated some worthy woman out of a profitable divorce.
Footloose and fiancée free.
A man who never makes the same mistake once.

Courtship   The period during which a girl decides whether or not she can do any better.

Divorce   When two people make a mistake and one person pays for it.

Husband   A guy who smiled back once too often.
What's left of a sweetheart after the nerve's been removed.

Intuition   That certain something, which tells a woman she's right …
whether she is or not.

Marriage   A broken engagement.
When deep, passionate love ripens into friendship.
A rest period between romances.

Pram   Last year's fun on wheels!

Sex   The poor man's polo.

Silly game   One you can beat your wife at.

The best man

STOP!

IF YOU HAVE JUST ARRIVED DIRECT FROM PAGE NINE,

BEFORE ATTEMPTING TO READ THIS CHAPTER,

DO YOURSELF A FAVOUR – RETURN TO PAGE ELEVEN.

As I said earlier in the book, the best man is expected to be the 'star of the show'. All too often, however, he is ill-equipped and ill-prepared. Sometimes, he's just ill.

By now, Mr Best Man, you should have learned enough to be able to give the guests a very pleasant surprise. If you've followed the guidelines, yours will stand out as a speech to remember – a wedding gift to the bride and groom and an entertainment for the crowd.

Let me remind you that you are officially replying to the groom on behalf of the bridesmaids. If there are no bridesmaids, I suggest that you regard yourself as speaking on behalf of the guests.

You may wish to tell the bridegroom's life story in some detail, ribbing him along the way. It's also quite nice to refer to news stories and world events that were taking place around the time of his birth. This technique helps to create interesting pictures in the minds of our audience and puts the bridegroom's life into a chronological perspective. You might like to use Google for your research. If the year in question is 1983 for instance, just enter '1983 events', and you'll be able to get all the information you need from Wikipedia, Infoplease, BBC and many others.

Don't make a meal of it. Your speech should only last around seven minutes, ten at the most.

In the following draft speech, I have cast the bridegroom's brother as best man. I find this to be the case in one in every three weddings.

Host and hostess, bride and bridegroom, ladies and gentlemen;

It's time for *me* to make a speech now and, quite frankly, there's not a whole lot you can do about that.

Firstly, on behalf of the bridesmaids, I'd like to thank the bridegroom for his kind words. You know, I had a feeling it was going to be difficult to follow a speech by my brother David and I was quite right …
I couldn't follow a bloody *word* of it!

I have to tell you that to be asked to act as best man today is a great privilege …
and *bloody* inconvenient!

I should emphasise that the description, 'Best Man', has absolutely nothing to do with the wedding night - but I will be standing by in case of emergencies.

This morning at the ceremony, I think everyone will agree … the bride looked absolutely stunning! …

(Pause for 'Hear hears' and possibly a ripple of applause.)

The groom looked absolutely stunned!

Incidentally, I must say that, personally, I regret the fact that the bride no longer says 'obey' in the marriage service.
It used to be the only real laugh in the whole ceremony!

Of course, there's no doubt, marriage is a wonderful invention …
but then, of course, so was the low-level flushing cistern!

Now I'm probably in a better position than most, to pay tribute to the groom …

after all, he's almost like a brother to me …
and I'm not going to stand up here this afternoon and
make cheap, obvious jokes about Dave …
let's face it, he deserves respect.

Dave Newberry is a man who knows where he's going …
and who knows where he's been …
He just doesn't know where he *is*!

He once left a note on his office door …
it said: 'Back in an hour' :
When he got back after lunch,
he saw the sign and sat down to wait!

He's not with us.

I honestly don't know what the hell I'm going to do
without my big brother …
and believe me, I just can't wait to find out!

But ladies and gentlemen, I've been asked today to
praise Dave, not to bury him …
Mind you, I must say, the vote was bloody close!

Dave has always been very fussy about his
appearance …
Now it isn't easy being a slave to fashion when one head
is missing off your bunny slippers …
but he does his best.

Today, we see before us a very presentable looking guy,
so it may surprise you to learn that it wasn't always that
way …
Dave was not a pretty baby.
Mother didn't get morning sickness until *after* he was
born!

Yes, our parents were a little disappointed when David came into the world …
they'd set their hearts on a golden retriever.

He was a slow starter …
he didn't even talk until he was nine years old.
Someone switched off the TV in the middle of 'Big Brother' and he said, 'Hey!'

By the time he was fourteen, Mum and Dad were very concerned about his performance at school …
he wasn't just falling behind,
he was getting lapped!

When friends asked them what they thought Dave would be when he left school,
they used to say: 'About thirty-five!'

My brother spent much of his teens trying to find himself.
Then one fateful day, he had a haircut …
and there he was!

Happily, as we all know, the lovely Miss Lucas came into his life and today, seeing Dave with his wonderful bride, I realise what a good choice he's made …
I really admire his taste …
which is more than I can say for *hers*!

Never mind, one thing's for sure …
with Lucy by his side, how can he possibly go wrong?

Lucy has some remarkable qualities, one of which – thank goodness – is a well-developed sense of humour.
She's a great sport. Lucy can really take a joke – and today, in front of witnesses – she did!
Of course, she'll also need quite a lot of patience …

Dave has one rather disturbing habit; he tends to keep putting things off. Yes, people have often accused him of being a procrastinator …

one of these days I'm sure he'll get around to denying it

but he certainly didn't *dare* to try to delay today's ceremony …

After all, he of all people should know how volatile Lucy can be. A few weeks ago, after a little disagreement they had, I watched her throw a pile of Dave's clothes straight out of the window.

Trouble was, he was *wearing* them at the time!

Ladies and gentlemen,

it's now my pleasant duty to thank Dave on behalf of the bridesmaids, Laura, Trudy and Angela, for his very kind words …

it's a real pleasure to act as spokesman for such a lovely team of ladies …

I'd also like to add my thanks to Elayne and Jack Lucas on behalf of all the guests for the hospitality we've enjoyed this afternoon.

Like everybody here, I wish Lucy and Dave all the happiness in the world.

As a man who'll drink to absolutely anything, I'd be very grateful if you would all give me an excuse to raise my glass again by joining me in one more toast to the happy couple …

and this piece of advice to my big brother … Dave …

'To keep your marriage brimming in the everloving cup –

whenever you're wrong, admit it …

whenever you're right; shut up!'

Ladies and gentlemen …

the new Mr and Mrs Newberry …

Lucy and Dave!

Extra lines suitable for the best man

Should a couple embarking on marriage be frank and earnest?
Or should one of them be a girl?

Show me a modern man who comes home every evening, is greeted with smiles and compliments, has his coat taken, his shoes removed, pillows arranged for him, made to feel comfortable and welcome in every way, then is served a really delicious meal …
and I'll show you a modern man who lives in a Japanese restaurant.

The bride wanted a very simple wedding, and that's what she got …
starting with the bridegroom.

At the last wedding I went to, the bride was so ugly …
everybody kissed the groom!

But marriage isn't for everyone …
men, for instance.

It only takes a couple of words mumbled in church and you're married.
It only takes a couple of words mumbled in your sleep and you're divorced.

Sex is no reason to get married …
unless you've lost interest in it.

By the way, I have some bad news for you Dave …
One of the waiters just brought Lucy a couple of aspirins.

Lucy wanted a formal wedding,
so her father painted the shotgun white!

Bigamy is having one wife too many …
monogamy is usually the same.

They have a wedding album, a wedding video, a
wedding book …
The Kyoto Conference didn't have coverage that good!

Scientists have a found a definite link between marriage,
sex and astrology …
if you've been married over twenty-five years, sex
happens once in a blue moon.

So now, Dave's career as a bachelor can be summed up
in one word …
over!

You may wish to incorporate into your speech a quotation on the
subject of marriage. Don't use more than one or two. You'll find some
near the end of this book.

Best man's advice to the bride and bridegroom

Hug and squeeze and kiss her daily …
and if her daily won't go along with it, try the au pair!

By the way, the best time to do the washing up is …
straight after she tells you to.

If you're clever,
you'll always have the last word.
If you're *really* clever, you won't use it.

Lucy, treat him like a dog …
three meals a day, plenty of affection and a loose leash.

If he ever threatens to leave you,
hold out for a firm promise!

Dave; don't be complacent. Keep a look-out for little tell-
tale signs of trouble in your relationship … like …
if you see the milkman wearing your socks.

I mean, you wouldn't want her having headaches with
another man would you?

No matter how she treats you, it's always a good idea to
try and look a little hurt.

It's always a good idea to get married early in the
morning.
That way, if it doesn't work out, you haven't wasted the
whole day!

Every now and then, try a little tenderness …
Sprinkle some monosodium glutamate on your beloved.

Never go to bed angry …
stay up and fight!

I'll tell you how much point there is in arguing with your
wife …
have you ever tried blowing out a lightbulb?

Marriage is something you have to work at, nurture,
add to …
you know, like a compost heap!

(Bridging line)

The big drinker

He's a drinker, but he's a happy drinker – always
laughing and shaking hands …
even when he's alone.

Just a few minutes ago the barman said to him: 'What
would you like to drink; brandy, gin, scotch, lager?'
He said: 'Yes.'

When I left him on his stag night, he was in the middle of
the High Street, trying to roll up the white line.

Ladies and gentlemen,
your bridegroom is a man of vision;
sometimes blurred, sometimes double!

I told him that vodka is a slow poison.
He said: 'I'm in no hurry.'

When he gave blood recently, his was the only
contribution with a head on it.

Here's the good news …
he's not drinking any more.
Here's the bad news …
he's not drinking any less.

He does fifty push-ups a day…
not intentionally, he just falls down a lot.

(Bridging line)

He was caught by the police under the new strict
breathalyser rules …
not only did he have to blow into the bag,
he then had to twist it into the shape of a kangaroo.

He was in a panic yesterday;
he lost the cork from his lunch.

When pink elephants get pissed, they see *him*!

What a party! I watched him for twenty minutes, trying to get a mini pizza into the CD player!

One weekend in London, he was found putting pennies into a sewer and looking up at Big Ben ...
he thought he was weighing himself.
(Bridging line)

He gets drunk on water ...
as well as on land.

The doctors gave him some tests and it turned out to be serious ...
they found blood in his alcohol system.
(Bridging line)

He gets pickled so often his nickname is 'Onions'.

He's a talented amateur magician ...
he can walk down the street and turn into a pub.
(Bridging line)

Fame at last ...
he's in the latest edition of 'Booze Who'.

When he's drinking spirits, there's no use in giving him a chaser ...
nothing's going to catch him.

He's always short of money. He can never manage to make both ends meet …
he's too busy making one end drink.

(Bridging line)

He only feels really fulfilled when he's really filled full!

Currently, his favourite tipple is a trendy new cocktail called 'Autumn Leaf' …
One sip and you change colour and fall to the ground!

I'll never forget the day he dropped a bottle of scotch on the floor …
I'd never seen so many splinters in a tongue!

What a man! …
I once saw him down two bottles of brandy and not once did he stagger.
Stagger? … He couldn't even bloody move!

He doesn't really remember how he met Lucy …
he just sobered up one morning and there she was!

(Bridging line)

Actually, he can't drink too much right now …
tonight's a big night and he doesn't want to take the risk …
Rumour has it that he's like a load of fireworks in November;
bloody useless after the fifth!

(Bridging line)

If Dracula bit him in the neck, he'd get a Bloody Mary!

The bore

I hate bores; they insist on talking about themselves when I want to talk about ME!

Here are some lines to roast 'em with …

He has that magic ability to light up a room …
as soon as he leaves it.

If you happen to see two guys together and one of them looks really bored …
he's the other.

You can always tell when he's talking rubbish …
his lips are moving!

He recently came down with 24-hour flu …
even a virus can't stand him any longer than that!

There's an old Chinese proverb:
'One picture is worth a thousand words' …
Dave Newberry never had that picture.

When you're in his company, believe me – there's never a dull moment …
it lasts all the way through.

Is he man of small calibre or just a big bore?

You know, if all the people who sat through one of Dave's stories were lined up three feet apart, they'd stretch …
That's it … they'd stretch.

I could really enjoy his conversation if it weren't for two things …
my ears!

Not only does he encroach on your time, he trespasses on eternity.

He'll be speaking next and I can assure you, he's really on form …
Chloroform!

He's the sort of conversationalist who leaves people gasping for *less*.

He never opens his mouth,
unless he has nothing to say.

He's a keen gardener;
he talks to his plants …
no wonder they droop … they're asleep!
(Bridging line)

They say is mind wanders a bit, but let's face it …
wouldn't yours if you were in that body?
(Bridging line)

God's gift (the ego has landed)

He's so vain, he ought to be in somebody's wrist.

Actually, I'm surprised he's not taking his own hand in marriage!

I'm sure he'll be a caring husband. I can see it now …
every night, he'll take her in his arms, hold her close …
and tell her how wonderful he is.

Some people marry for love …
some people marry for companionship …
Dave got married because he wanted to see his name printed on little matchboxes.

One time he almost drowned, and God's life flashed before his eyes.

He says that if there's such a thing as reincarnation, he's coming back as himself!

He told me he's a self-made man …
naturally, I accepted his apology.

His prized possession is on his desk, inscribed:
'To the greatest guy I know' …
and, let me tell you,
I've never seen a mirror so well polished!

At one time he wanted to join the Navy …
He wanted to join the Navy to let the world see *him*!

His three favourite forms of entertainment are radio,
television …
and mirrors.

He's so conceited, he sends his mother congratulations
on *his* birthday.

If this guy's on an ego trip,
he must be travelling very light!

It's just as well he's not wearing an open-neck shirt
tonight;
he's covered in love bites …
all self-inflicted, of course.

But there's a lot to be said for Dave Newberry …
and he's usually the one that's saying it.

He certainly knows a good thing when he sees it …
in the mirror.

He never has an unkind word to say about anyone …
mostly because he only talks about himself.

The happy couple

When the bride and bridegroom have been living together for some time, the usual 'new home', 'new beginning', 'married bliss' crap doesn't work. Some of the following lines may be a little more realistic. (Nevertheless, there's also a bit of crap in case you need it.)

They're such a busy couple;
he's never found her in and she's never found him out.

They've worked out a great way of settling arguments:
he admits he's wrong,
and she admits she's right.

They're a fastidious couple.
Lucy's fast and Dave's hideous.

We have here, two good God-fearing people who
observe the Ten Commandments …
five each.

Of course they have their little scraps, but never anything
very serious …
nothing three police sergeants and a couple of
paramedics can't sort out.

They go together like Teflon and Velcro.

I've been asked to deny the rumour that they met when
they were both having sex-change operations.

Lucy and Dave share a sense of humour …
they *have* to share it;
he hasn't got one of his own.

They have a pre-nuptial agreement …
nothing complicated –
he's going to wash and she's going to dry.

He's a bit stupid and she's always on a diet …
That's why they'll stay together through thick and thin.
(Bridging line)

They married for better and for worse;
he couldn't have done better,
she couldn't have done worse.

So now, Dave is married to a wonderful person.
Unfortunately, Lucy's not that lucky.

He proposed to her on his hands and knees …
he had to, she was under the table at the time.
(Bridging line)

Lucy and Dave have slightly different priorities:
she wants their marriage to work
and he wants *her* to work.

They fix breakfast together;
she makes the toast and he scrapes it.
(Bridging line)

The honeymoon

So off they go tomorrow for their honeymoon in
Marbella …
God knows how Dave's going to hold his stomach in for
two solid weeks.

(Bridging line)

Why is it they're flying hundreds of miles to get away
from people just so they can spend half their
honeymoon writing out cards that say…
'Wish you were here'?

They're booked in to a place that's pretty unusual for a
Spanish hotel …
it's finished.

It's so far off the beaten track,
the crow doesn't even fly there.

I don't want to spoil it for them,
but I know that hotel.
It was mentioned in the 'Michelin Guide' …
It said: 'Don't!'

It's such a dump …
Kate Adie stands in front of it and pretends to be giving
live coverage from Basra.

I must tell you Lucy and Dave, in the bathrooms, the
walls are full of cracks …
mind you, you've probably heard most of them.

Lucy's had a special sign made to hang on the outside of
their hotel bedroom door: 'Please disturb!'

Hypochondriacs

When I think of Dave Newberry, I think of champagne …
Every pain he has is a sham.

He's so full of penicillin,
every time he sneezes he cures someone.

I've got a great wedding present for him – it costs £300
and comes in a chest …
pneumonia.

This is a very sick man
in a perfectly healthy body.

He's suffering from Seven Dwarfs Flu …
he's sleepy, sneezy, dopey, bashful and grumpy,
and he won't be happy until he goes to see Doc.

When Dave was a kid and his mother was offering round
the Smarties, she had to tell him they were pills.

If the truth be known,
this guy's not stricken – he's chicken!

Wanna spoil his day?
Just tell him how healthy he looks.

He takes no chances;
he has an annual check-up every week.

It was very moving this morning in church …
Lucy recited her vows …
Dave recited his symptoms.

(Bridging line)

He's the only guy I ever met who could tell me exactly how many measles he had.

The way he starts whingeing when he gets a little cold, there's no way of knowing whether to call a doctor or a drama critic.

I'm single – ha! ha!

For those of you who don't know,
I'm not actually married;
I just look this way because I've been ill!

I admit that as a bachelor I have no real idea of what it
feels like to be happily married …
But then, of course, nor do most husbands!

Being single means you don't have to leave a party just
as you're starting to have a good time.

I often think of marriage myself;
it keeps my mind off sex!

I had this beautiful Sicilian girlfriend once …
She had a face that could break your heart,
and an uncle who could break your legs.

She lived on the other side of the street,
but she finally came across.

I've never been married but I think I know what it must
be like;
I tried to get out of a book club once.

When I get married,
it's going to be the real thing – sex!

Difference between a girlfriend and a wife: 43 pounds.
Difference between a boyfriend and a husband: 43
minutes.

Infuriating and aggressive

Use these lines for the guy who quite enjoys being thought of as tough, ruthless and nasty. More gentle insults may be found under 'Put-downs (Various)'.

Ladies and gentlemen,
if there's anybody here this afternoon who feels strangely nervous and apprehensive …
it's probably because you just went and married Dave Newberry.

Now, nobody knows what made Mr Newberry so bloody infuriating …
but whatever it was, it worked!

He's so infuriating that, when he was fifteen years old, his *parents* ran away from home.

He's so infuriating that, on a visit to Canada, a load of baby seals got together and clubbed *him*!

He's so infuriating that once, in Switzerland, he climbed a mountain, called out his own name …
and the echo said, 'Jump!'

I'm one of his oldest friends …
he can't *get* new ones.

He's been described as conceited, selfish, arrogant and insensitive …
and let's face it, a mother should know!

I *was* going to say he's his own worst enemy,
but I forgot about me.

His idea of fun is to sneak into Claridges and put piranha
fish in the finger bowls.

He's got a split personality ...
and I don't like either of them.

People who have known him for some time have formed
their own support group.

Yes, there's only one Dave Newberry ...
but then, of course, there was only one Hiroshima!

His personality is such that he can walk into the room
and immediately make strangers.

He hasn't got many faults,
but he makes the most of the ones he has.

I wouldn't say he's a prat,
but he'll certainly do until one comes along.

Still ... he's a nice guy deep down ...
and sometimes, that's where I wish he was.

Lazy

Dave has never been the type to sit in the office
watching the clock, waiting for half-past-five …
He leaves at *four*!

He's due to go into hospital shortly …
they have to remove something from his backside …
a chair.

Around the office this man is like God;
he's rarely seen, he's holier than thou, and if he does
anything it's considered a bloody miracle!

He has this driving, insistent, irresistible, aggressive
compulsion to do absolutely nothing.

His job means he's able to work eight hours and sleep
eight hours …
Trouble is, they're the same eight hours.

They tell me he had his window box paved over!

He says he's superstitious …
he won't do any work during a week that has a Friday
in it.

He's certainly not afraid of work;
he fights against it like a tiger!

He's a late riser; in fact, until recently he didn't realise
there were two eight o'clocks in the same day.

Naïve

He's always been rather naïve when it comes to sexual matters …

he actually believes that mutual climax is an insurance company!

She thinks Spanish Fly is something on the front of King Juan Carlos's trousers.

He thinks the menopause is a control button on his DVD player.

Someone told him the most important thing in sex is foreplay …

so he invited another couple.

She's a bit naïve when it comes to politics.

When I asked her opinion of Red China, she said it looks best on a white tablecloth.

He's just as bad …

when I asked him if he's a right-winger or a left-winger …

he said he prefers the drumsticks.

Occupations

Accountant   They gave him a key job at KPMG …

he has to lock up at night.

Actor   During the ceremony, he made it very obvious he was an actor. When the vicar said: 'Do you take this woman to be your lawful wedding wife?' …

he paused, then whispered: 'Line?'

Advertising   The nice thing about the advertising business is that it really keeps you fit;

every lunch hour you're out looking for another job.

Architect   He had designs on the boss's wife.

Banker   He's always being asked for his advice. Obviously, people are too bloody lazy to come up with their own ideas for losing money.

Boss   He's a very progressive employer. He simply can't bear to see his secretary doing all that tedious work, so he usually goes off and has a drink.

Church   He didn't make it as a priest …

he kept giggling during the last rites.

Circus   The whole show went to Birmingham in a specially chartered bus …

all except the contortionist; he went under his own auspices.

Dentist	If a dentist breaks a dental mirror in your mouth, do you get seven years of bad teeth?
Doctor	She so jealous, she listens in on his stethoscope.
Electrician	He made a fortune in Amsterdam … he was an electrician in the red-light district.
Estate agent	Business was so quiet that he sat around most of the time, playing Monopoly with his partners, and guess what … none of the houses sold!
Hairdresser	She had to close up the business because she just couldn't make split ends meet.
Law student	For a girl studying law, she didn't put up much of a defence.
Lawyer	It's a mixed marriage … he's a lawyer and she's a human being.
Musician	He's technically fantastic! He never hits a wrong note … never makes a mistake … it's amazing! … all that crap is quite deliberate.
Office work	It takes him half an hour to get to work every day … after he gets to his desk.

Publishing	For a time, he worked for the publisher of a thesaurus ...
	Then one day, he was fired, canned, dismissed, let go, dispensed with, discharged ...
Salesman	For a time he went round door-to-door, selling 'knock knock' jokes.
Stockbroker	Last week, he bought shares in Pfizer, the company that manufactures Viagra. Sure enough, one hour later, they went up.
Teacher	Most teachers take up the profession for two reasons ...
	July and August.
Undertaker	He learned his craft in California, working for a mortician whose slogan was: 'Have a nice death.'
Unemployed	He goes for a lot of interviews ...
	his CV is in its fifth reprint.

Overweight

This guy has the body of a twenty-year-old …
A twenty-year-old *Volvo*!

No man is an island …
but Dave Newberry comes pretty close.

The poor bloke suffers from stomach trouble;
he can't get his trousers over it!

Actually, that isn't really his stomach …
he's just got a low chest.

He used to be worse …
at one point he got so fat,
his belly button unravelled itself.

He's got a sunken living room at home.
He didn't plan it that way, it just happened.

They say there are three men to every woman in this town;
Looks like Lucy got hers all in one lump.

Yes, at first glance he may look a little heavy,
but don't let that fool you;
he's quite capable of touching his toes …
only with his belly, but it's a start!

(Bridging line)

But he's in shape …
the *wrong* shape.

He weighs in at twelve-four …
on the Richter Scale!

The first time I met him, he was standing on the corner
of Oxford Street …
and Fulham High Road.

He was wearing an all-green suit.
He looked like the Cotswolds with lapels.

He does wonderful impressions …
He eats like a pig and drinks like a fish.

(Bridging line)

He always used to say he was saving himself for when
the right girl came along …
Did he have to save so much?

He claims to be a light eater. He is …
As soon as it gets light he starts eating!

As it happens, he's very conscious of his diet.
Every day he eats something from one of the four main
food groups …
McDonalds, Burger King, Wimpy and Kentucky Fried
Chicken!

Yes, for him a balanced meal means …
a Big Mac in each hand!

His idea of pumping iron is lifting a knife, fork and
spoon!

(Bridging line)

He's obsessed with food …
This is a guy who always puts his stomach first;
especially when going through a door.

He hasn't an ounce of excess flesh on his body …
he's got *pounds* of it!

He got hit by a Smart Car once …
it took three surgeons to remove it.

He's certainly got a good head on his shoulders …
mind you, it would look better on a *neck*.
(Bridging line)

This guy's had more hot dinners …
than you've had hot dinners.

He's so fat,
they've made him a honorary suburb.

He tried to run away from home once when he was a
kid, but the fridge was too heavy.

This man is not only larger than life,
he's also larger than his own trousers.
(Bridging line)

No wonder his stomach looks like a beer barrel …
it is!
(Bridging line)

She's eating for two …
herself and Newcastle-upon-Tyne.

She had the mumps for two weeks before anybody noticed it.

They say she has a lot of cellulite. I don't believe it.
I mean, just because a blind man once tried to read her arse …

Put-downs (various)

He didn't get where he is today by luck …
he had to fight and claw his way to the bottom.

Here's a man who started out with nothing …
and he still has most of it.

He may *seem* insignificant, but there's a lot less to him than meets the eye.

Some people need no introduction …
Dave Newberry needs all the introduction he can get.

Words cannot express my feelings for this man …
but *fingers* can!
(Make a 'V' sign towards victim.)

This man knows exactly where he's going …
and where he's been …
he just doesn't know where he *is*!

Look at him! …
maybe we can freeze him until we find a cure.

His father looks upon him as the son he never had.

He's a man of hidden talent.
As soon as we find one, we'll let you know.

Dave Newberry could be described as charming,
intelligent and entertaining …
and perhaps one day, he *will* be.

Nobody thinks more highly of him than I do,
and that'll give you some idea, 'cos I think he's a prat!

He's not an easy man to ignore, but if you possibly can,
it's well worth the effort.

Here is a man who has taken dignity, sound judgement
and good taste …
and thrown them right out of the window!

He's working on his second million …
he gave up on his first.

When they made Dave Newberry,
they kept the mould and threw *him* away.

Some people are one in a million …
Dave Newberry was won in a raffle.

He may *look* stupid,
but that doesn't mean he's not.

He seems too good to be true …
he isn't.

He's a man of hidden shallows.

Here's a guy who started his career at the bottom …
and *stayed* there!

But he's unpredictable;
just as you begin to figure out what makes him tick …
he begins to tock!

In business, he has a very sophisticated technique for
decision making …
'Eenie, meeenie, miney, mo!'.

Unfettered by ability, unhindered by style, unimpeded by
talent, this man is *above* professionalism …
he is in a category of his own …
crap.

He's bilingual …
unfortunately, neither language appears to be English!

Short

But I'm not going to stand up here and make fun of my
friend;
life's too short …
and so is Dave.

The Newberrys are all the same …
his family tree is a *stump*!

You see, they just don't make guys like him any longer.

He was offered a part-time job once …
standing around in a bar …
they reckoned he made the drinks look bigger.

He's very superstitious …
he thinks it's unlucky to walk under a black cat.

He's a lumberjack …
for bonsai trees.

Sports

Bowling	He's a tough guy … when he goes ten-pin bowling, he bowls overarm.
Boxing	During his career, they threw the towel in so many times, he opened his own linen service.
Cricket	This all started when he was a little boy and his father bought him a bat for his birthday. Imagine his surprise when he unwrapped it … and it flew away.
Fishing	Here's to our fisherman bold, Here's to the fish he caught, Here's to the one that got away … And here's to the one he bought!
Golf	Ah yes! Give me some golf clubs, some fresh air and a beautiful woman … and you can *keep* the bloody clubs and fresh air!
Motor sport	His main hobby is drag racing … and, let's face it, it isn't easy jumping hurdles in a cocktail dress.
Parachute	It's a tough sport … you jump out of a plane at fifteen thousand feet, aim for a little black dot on the ground and, if you don't pull the ripcord in time, that little black dot is you!

Referees	You know the trouble with referees? …
	They don't give a toss who wins!
Rugby	Playing rugby is a great way to meet new people …
	paramedics, nurses, orthopaedic surgeons …
Running	I prefer sex …
	it's much more fun and you don't need special shoes!
Soccer	The team is just like an old-fashioned bra …
	no cups and poor support.
Scuba diving	He had a narrow escape last year …
	something went wrong and Jacques Cousteau's life passed before his eyes.
Skiing	Skiing's easy …
	I learned in just ten sittings.
Table tennis	The recreation room was so small, you couldn't even play 'ping-pong' …
	all you could play was 'ping'.
Tennis	He has a serve that *no one* can return …
	it always hits the net first!

The wimp

I feel confident Lucy will never leave him …
she's spent too much time training the poor sod.

He's never been married before …
he's a self-made mouse.

Did you notice? When the vicar asked:
'Do you take this woman?', Lucy said:
'He does!'

He'll never forget the day he proposed to her …
it was the first time he's ever had his way of
kneeling criticised.

He's spent so much time buttering-up his future father-
in-law, he's developed a cholesterol problem.

He's a mild, inoffensive man …
but then, of course, so was Crippen.

Poor bloke, even on his honeymoon he's gonna have to
play his cards right.

When he gets into a lift, he says: 'Fourth floor please …
as long it doesn't take you out of your way.'

You know, he used to be a stunt man on 'Songs of
Praise'.

He's very loyal in his relationships; when he was a kid
and he used to go out walking with his mum…
he never ever looked at other mums.

Last year on holiday there was this bully on the beach,
trying to push him around …
He didn't take it lying down …
he got his own back on her grandchildren!

The older man

A word of warning Lucy –
you'll have to make a few allowances.
At his age, his back goes out more often than *he* does.

Don't be fooled by that healthy glow …
it's not a sun tan …
it's just that all his liver spots have grown together.

Longevity runs in his family …
when his grandfather died, he was pushing a hundred
and three! …
Mind you, that was on the M6!

Have you heard about his drug habit? …
He snorts Phyllosan!

I'm looking forward to those long, summer nights when
we can all go over to their place and sit round the table
listening to the sound of his arteries hardening.

I bet their first baby looks just like Dave …
all wrinkled and bald.

(Bridging line)

He went to school in the days before History was a
subject.

After the speeches you may wish to shake the
bridegroom's hand,
but there's really no need …
at his age, just *hold* his hand and it'll shake all by itself.

Despite his age, Dave Newberry has quite a lot going …
His hair's going, his liver's going, his teeth are going …

But really, he doesn't look forty …
not any more.

He still likes the good life, even at his age …
look at him, sitting there casually sipping his pruna
colada.

I know his blood type has been deleted from the
catalogue, but …

The three ages of men …
under age, over age and average.

The pregnant bride

It happens a lot today. When the bride is pregnant, it's usually pretty obvious to everyone anyway, so provided folks are comfortable with the situation (especially the bride), here are some lines …

> He proposed with those four magic words, four time-honoured words that led them to the altar ...
> 'You're not, are you?'

> This wedding proves once and for all that opposites attract …
> she's pregnant and he isn't.

> It's been a typical love story;
> at first she got his goat …
> now she's carrying his kid!

> I don't know if you noticed this, but at the ceremony she didn't say 'I do', she said 'I did'!

> I really don't want to comment on just how hastily this wedding took place, but why did Lewis Hamilton drive them to the church?

> It's important that a newly married couple are able to make ends meet …
> come to think of it, that's why they had to get married.
> (Bridging line)

> He proposed to her in a restaurant and it was very sudden. Right out of the blue.
> It was just after she ordered a mushroom, pickle and chocolate pizza.

This was a shotgun wedding ...
it made history; it's the first time the shotgun was
pointed at the woman!

By the way, let me read you an excerpt from 'Tips for
First-time Parents':
Tip number 34: *All* newborn babies are wrinkled.
Do *not* try to iron them!

Remember; everything that goes into a baby's mouth has
to be boiled first ...
which probably explains why so few mothers breast-
feed.

Apparently, due to Health Service cuts, there's a shortage
of women who deliver babies ...
a midwife crisis.

The serial bridegroom

Here are some lines with which to rib the previously married bridegroom. A word of warning; make sure the bride is a good sport about his past and, in any case, don't overdo it. Use two lines at most.

Dave Newberry is a man who signs his wedding certificate in pencil.

This guy's been up and down the aisle more often than Jerry Springer!

His last marriage was like schoolwork;
when they met it was chemistry …
then it turned to biology …
now … it's history.

Some guys get married for money,
some guys get married for love;
this guy gets married for spite!

His top priority has always been finding the right woman to have his children …
because – frankly – he was fed up with 'em!

But he's really a wonderful man, a charitable man.
Whenever he comes across a worthy cause …
he marries it!

Here's the good news, Lucy …
It's been said that what he lacks in size, he makes up for in quickness.
Here's the bad news, Lucy …
It was his last wife who said it!

I've been to a lot of weddings in my time …
and most of them have been his.

They don't issue him with a new wedding licence any more …
they just punch the old one.

He's been married so many times,
he has a direct debit account at Caxton Hall.

He's the only guy I know who *leases* his wedding rings from Aspreys!

The last time, he married for better and for worse …
but not for long!

His wedding certificate reads:
'To whom it may concern'.

Once bitten, twice broke.

It's better to have love and lust
then never to have love at all.

The bride

The days of blushing, virginal brides have all but disappeared. No longer are women considered to be mere appendages to their menfolk. They run businesses, they negotiate, they travel. Very often they are better paid than their husbands.

The bride's speech, once a rarity, may now be here to stay.

Or not.

Either way, here are some suitable lines …

> Mum and dad, Janice and Allen, family and friends, ladies and gentlemen …
> I think it's about time you heard from the female of the speeches!
>
> I have to admit I'm a bit nervous today. It must be something I married!
>
> If I'd only known that getting involved with Dave Newberry would lead to my having to stand up in public to make a speech, I can assure you I'd never have answered his advert.
>
> You see, making a speech is very much like having a baby;
> it's fun to conceive, but hell to deliver!
>
> But, I really wanted to add my thanks to all of you for coming today to help us celebrate our happiness.
> Of course, when it comes to happiness, how could we possibly fail?
> For a start, we're both very much in love with the bridegroom.

As most of you know, my David is not the kind of man to be tortured with self-worth problems.
He once asked me to rate him as a lover, on a scale of nine to ten.

But I must say, this lovely man has given me some of the best minutes of my life!

On this very special day, tradition dictates that the bride has with her – something old, something true, something borrowed and something blue...
but enough about the bridegroom's liver!

He tricked me into marrying him ...
he told me I was pregnant!

In my experience, there are three types of men:
the intelligent, the sensitive and the majority.

In Dave Newberry, I've found myself a real 'go-getter'.
Actually, I'd have preferred an already-got, but you can't have everything.

The trouble with a husband who works like a horse is that all he wants to do in the evenings is hit the hay.

Remember, behind every successful man, there's usually a woman telling him he's not so hot.

We have a very enlightened vicar. Did you hear him this morning? 'Do you take this man for better ...
or probably worse?'

Husbands are all very much alike...
they just have different faces so you can tell them apart.

My fantasy is to have two men at the same time …
one cleaning, one ironing.

Some husbands come in handy around the house.
Others come in unexpectedly!

It wasn't exactly a proposal as such. He took me out to a
Chinese restaurant for a romantic meal and asked: 'How
would you like your rice, fried or steamed?'
I looked him in the eye and whispered: 'Thrown!'

My policy is to let him think he's going to be bossing the
house …
when actually he's going to be housing the boss!

Husbands are like old kerosene lamps …
They're not particularly bright …
They often get turned down …
They smoke all day …
And they go out at night.

➤   Choosing a husband is exactly like choosing a house …
you ignore the way it is and picture how it's going to be
once you've got it remodelled.
(Bridging line)

Women have a higher threshold of pain …
and when they get married, men carry them over it.

'Some women get all excited about nothing …
and then marry him.'
(Goldie Hawn)

Give a man a free hand and he'll run it all over you.
(Mae West)

Guns don't kill people …
husbands who come home too early kill people!

If all his previous girlfriends were laid end to end,
I wouldn't be at all surprised.

But I'm really looking forward to married life with Dave.
Of course, there'll have to be a few adjustments, certain
activities will have to go: football on Saturday afternoons,
rugby every Sunday, getting hammered with the boys
down the pub – I'm really going to have to cut down on
all that!

Women have many faults,
Men have only two;
Everything they bloody say
And everything they do.

Appendages

Selected extras that may be appropriate.

The sincerity section

Oh God! I've been dreading this!

Here are some words to counterbalance the roast lines and cynical gags. Included are some 'positive' one-liners: humorous words of flattery useful for guys and gals who just can't take the other stuff. Some of the guests may actually enjoy listening to this tosh and, in any case, if your speech is packed only with zingers, it'll be all 'ping' and no 'pong'. So let's get it over with, shall we?

> To the bride and bridegroom we pledge fifty years of happiness.
> Invite us back for your Golden Wedding and we'll be delighted to renew that pledge.

> Lucy ...
> please remember that Dave is yours on approval.
> You may return him for credit or exchange,
> but your love will not be refunded.

> A marriage may be made in Heaven,
> but the maintenance work has to be carried out here on Earth.

> Love grouts wrinkles.

> They say that behind every successful man is an astonished mother-in-law ...
> When Dave's success comes ... and it will ... nobody is going to be surprised, least of *all* his mother-in-law.

> (Bridging line)

She's a very well-educated girl, speaks several languages.
Not only can this young lady read the bottom line of the
eye-testing chart, she can pronounce it!

He's all-man … he knows no fear!
He came into the world as a creature of adventure …
the first thing he did when he was born was to bungee
jump with his umbilical cord.

Everybody loves her … she's a real charmer.
She has such a wonderful personality that when she
takes a taxi, the driver gives *her* a tip.

When it comes to food and drink, he's a real connoisseur.
He can tell from one sip of wine, not only the year it was
made …
not only the vineyard …
but he can tell you the bust measurement of the bird
who jumped on the bloody grapes!

Merely to call him a computer engineer is like calling
Michelangelo a decorator.

See also 'Love and marriage quotations'.

(Hey Madame Editor, do I have to keep writing this stuff?)

Yes. (Ed.)

Illness and bereavement

There's always a danger, when handling certain sensitive issues such as serious illness or recent bereavement, that your audience will become sombre and that your speech will end on a sad and awkward note.

The loss of a dear one has to be acknowledged by at least one of the speakers, and he risks losing his audience during what would otherwise have been a sparkling, laugh-a-minute speech. It's almost enough to make you wish they hadn't passed away, isn't it?

I always place these subjects about three-quarters of the way through the speech, giving the speech-maker plenty of time to ease out of the poignant atmosphere and back, gently, into the laughter.

Of course, the language you use is crucial. Avoid words like 'dead', 'killed', 'injured', 'terminal', etc. and substitute gentler language. Try to portray the departed with a semblance of continuity; here's an example:

> You know, it takes an occasion like this, when our close family and our good friends are with us, to remind us once again of those who can't be with us …
>
> among them, our dear Grandma who passed away last year, and who really would have enjoyed seeing Dave get hitched …
>
> And we all remember Dave's late partner and best friend, Sean, who we lost in August and is sadly missed.
>
> Sean would have been best man today and I'm proud to step in for him …
>
> in a way, I feel we're sharing the job.
>
> In any case, Dave was *my* best man two years ago so at last I can get my own back!

However tragic the circumstances of Sean's death, you'll notice that, while not in any way trivialising his passing, the words are totally natural and he is treated in a straightforward manner … almost as if he were on holiday.

This way, we've shown respect and affection to our absent friends, we've kept the audience from sinking into depression and we're ready to go straight into another series of one-liners before closing the speech.

Here's another example of how bereavement may be handled, including a mention of Aunt Fiona's surviving husband … In a way, I'm saying: 'Max made the effort and pulled himself together especially for today.' The lines, you'll notice, get lighter gradually so that you don't have an unseemly leap from sadness to hilarity.

> It really is nice to see so many of both families here today, but we all miss one very special lady, Aunt Fiona …
>
> she would have been very proud to be at Dave's wedding and we all think of her with love on this special occasion. However, we're delighted to welcome Uncle Max, who came along even though he knew full well that I'd be making a speech today. What a sport!
>
> Tonight the happy couple leave for their honeymoon in Cyprus. As many of you know, when Lucy goes abroad, she likes to learn about local dialects and customs …
>
> I hear that last time Lucy was in Cyprus, she picked up a little Greek …
>
> I hope she doesn't run into him; it might be quite embarrassing.

and so on …

Treat all illnesses as transient. This doesn't mean you should belittle other people's health problems, but bear in mind that each sufferer handles his or her condition differently.

Be safe. Acknowledge it, but don't dwell on it …

This sort of thing should be fine:

> We're all very happy to see Brenda here this afternoon, looking so well after her recent operation.

(Expect applause.)

Brenda, we're really delighted you were able to make it today and that you're obviously well on the road to recovery.

In a marquee

Ladies and gentlemen,
first of all, I must say what a thrill it is to be making a speech in a room that used to be Vanessa Feltz's nightie.

Welcome to the marquee ...
de Sade!

The last time I made a speech in a marquee,
I was so funny I brought the tent down.

My uncle used to be in the tent business,
but it folded.

Ladies and gentlemen,
welcome to Colonel Ghaddafi's time-share!

Toasts

A toast is a brilliant device; it flatters an ego, it closes a speech and it gives you an excuse to have a drink.

> Here's to the lasses we've loved, lad
> Here's to the lips we've pressed
> For kisses and lasses, like liquor in glasses
> The last is always the best!

(Don't be surprised if the audience shouts: 'Boom Boom!')

> Here's champagne to our real friends
> and real pain to our sham friends.

> Here's to happy days …
> any twit can have a good time at night.

> May you live as long as you want to
> and want to as long as you live!

> Here's to my mother-in-law's daughter,
> And here's to her father-in-law's son,
> And here's to the vows we've just taken,
> And the life we've just begun.

> Here's to the prettiest, here's to the wittiest,
> Here's to the truest of all who are true.
> Here's to the neatest one, here's to the sweetest one,
> Here's to them all in one … here's to you.

> Grow old along with me,
> The best is yet to be,
> I've got a credit card,
> Between us we've got three.

(With apologies to Herbert V. Prochnow)

Family and friends, here's looking at you …
which is why I need this drink!

Here's to our wives and sweethearts.
May our sweethearts become our wives,
and our wives ever remain our sweethearts.

(Puke! Puke!)

To long life and happiness …
Your long life will be our happiness.

Here's to love …
the only game where one pair beats three of a kind.

Here's to love …
the only fire for which there's no insurance.

Finally, this is what I call a 'groast' …

it's a cross between Grace and a Toast …

Lord … bless this bunch
while they munch lunch.

Heckling

Night club comics often have to cope with loud-mouth drunks and various nasty customers. The comedian is usually well-armed with several lines designed to turn the tables on the smart-ass and to get an extra laugh or two at the heckler's expense.

At a wedding, however, any heckling is usually very good-natured and restrained. It would be rather heavy-handed, if not churlish, for a wedding speaker to learn professional anti-heckler lines simply for the purpose of silencing someone enjoying the party.

So here they are …

> Feel free to speak your mind …
> I have a spare three seconds.

> You know you shouldn't really drink
> on an empty head!

> Nice suit …
> were you there for the fitting?

> Hey, I always wondered what became of that kid who
> played the banjo in 'Deliverance'.

> Look at him:
> the Ghost of Christmas Stupid!

> Did you ever get the feeling that Snow White and Dopey
> had a baby?

> I couldn't agree with you more …
> In fact, I couldn't agree with you at all!

> Hi there! And you certainly are!

Nice to see your voice is working.
Shame it's not connected to anything.

Isn't she a treasure?
I wonder who dug her up.

Hey! I thought alcoholics were meant to be anonymous!

Is there a new life-form out there that we don't yet know about?

Oh well, every village has one.

Love and marriage quotations

A mixed bag of quotes – some original, some borrowed – ranging from the sickeningly sincere to the seriously cynical.

Final score: Cynical: 22 Sincere: 10.

All the world loves a lover.
Except my girlfriend's husband.

It isn't premarital sex if you have no intention of getting married.

(George Burns)

Marriage is a novel where the hero dies in the first chapter.

A man is incomplete until he's married.
Then he's really finished.

Love works miracles every day; it weakens the strong and strengthens the weak ...
it makes fools of the wise and wises up the fools ...
it heightens passion, destroys reason and turns everything topsy turvy.

(Adapted from a quote by Marguerite de Valois)

Marriage halves our griefs, doubles our joys and quadruples our expenses.

Marriage is an armed alliance against the outside world.

(G. K. Chesterton)

The best and most beautiful things in the world cannot be seen or even touched. They must be felt with the heart.

(Helen Keller)

Marriage is the process where love ripens into vengeance.

One flesh.

(John Milton)

Marriage is like a dull meal with the dessert at the beginning.

(Pierre La Mure)

Many a man in love with a dimple makes the mistake of marrying the whole girl.

The first union to defy management.

(Will Rogers)

If you have half a mind to get married; do it! … that's all it takes!

An institution that turns a night owl into a homing pigeon.

(Glenn Shelton)

A wedding is very much like a funeral, except you smell your own flowers.

A man should not insult his wife publicly, at parties. He should insult her in the privacy of the home.

(James Thurber)

Marriage is an institution.
Marriage is love.
Love is blind.
Therefore, marriage is an institution for the blind.

The sort of woman who could make a fool out of a man could also make a man out of a fool.

Love is like quicksilver in the hand.
Leave the fingers open and it stays.
Clutch it, and it darts away.

(Dorothy Parker)

Love is like a curry …
you really have to have confidence in it to enjoy it.

The only life sentence that gets quashed by *bad* behaviour.

The surest way to save a marriage from divorce is not to show up for the wedding.

Thirty-five percent of marriages end in divorce.
The other sixty-five percent fight it out to the bitter end.

When it comes to relationships,
Love is the quest …
Seduction, the conquest …
Marriage, the inquest.

A deal in which a man gives away half his groceries in order to get the other half cooked.

(John Gwynne)

Marriage is very much like a pair of shears; joined together so that they can't be separated, often moving in opposite directions, yet always punishing anyone who comes between them.

(Some old twit)

Many marriages follow a set pattern;
first comes the engagement ring;
then comes the wedding ring;
then comes the suffering.

Marriages are made in heaven …
divorces are handled by a lower court.

Marriage is like a violin …
when the beautiful music is over, the strings are still
attached.

Marriage, after all, is not a lottery …
you've got a chance in a lottery!

Marriage is nature's way of keeping people from fighting
with strangers.

Most girls seem to marry men who happen to be like
their fathers.
Maybe that's why so many mothers cry at weddings.

Closing message

Well ... this is where I end the book because I'm sick of it now. There's just no way I can win. If your speech is a brilliant success, you certainly won't tell people you got it from a book, will you? Naah ... you'll take all the credit yourself, won't you? If it doesn't work, you'll probably write me a letter of complaint and embarrass me in front of my publishers.

Good luck with it anyway.

Now leave me alone.

Mitch Murray

Index

memorising speeches 24
microphones 27
Milton, John 120
mother-in-law one-liners 42–3
motor sport 97
musicians 88

'naïve' one-liners 86
notes for speeches 23

occupational one-liners
  accountants 87
  actors 87
  advertising business 87
  architects 87
  bankers 87
  bosses 87
  church and clergy 87
  circuses 87
  dentists 88
  doctors 88
  electricians 88
  estate agents 88
  hairdressers 88
  law students 88
  lawyers 88
  musicians 88
  office workers 88
  publishing 89
  salesmen 89
  stockbrokers 89
  teachers 89
  undertakers 89
  unemployment 89
office workers 88
older bridegrooms 100–1
openers 33–4
order of speeches 11–12
overweight 90–3

paper for speechwriting 24
parachuting 97
Parker, Dorothy 121

'ping-pong' method 35–8, 46
'positive' one-liners 110–11
practising 25
pram (definition) 61
pregnant brides 102–3
Prochnow, Herbert V. 115
programme order 11–12
publishing 89

quotations 119–22

reading technique 25–6
referees 98
reminiscences 16
rhythm and style 15–19
risqué material 30–1
Rogers, Will 120
rugby 98
running 98

salesmen 89
scuba diving 98
serial bridegroom 104–5
'set ups' and 'stings' 22
sex (definition) 61
Shelton, Glenn 120
'short' one-liners 96
silly game (definition) 61
sincerity section 110–11
soccer 98
soundbites 13
speeches
  length of 13, 62
  memorising 24
  notes for 23
  order of 11–12
  reading technique 25–6
  rhythm and style 15–19
  writing out 24–5
sports one-liners 97–8
  bowling 97
  boxing 97
  cricket 97